On the Farm

Goats
Nannies, Billies, and Kids

Lorijo Metz

PowerKiDS press
New York

To Georgia, who is clever, curious, and always goes her own way

Published in 2011 by The Rosen Publishing Group, Inc.
29 East 21st Street, New York, NY 10010

First Edition

Editor: Amelie von Zumbusch
Book Design: Greg Tucker
Photo Researcher: Jessica Gerweck

Photo Credits: Cover, pp. 4, 5, 6, 8, 9, 10, 11, 12, 13, 14, 15, 17, 19, 21, 22 Shutterstock.com; p. 7 © www.iStockphoto.com/Bobbi Gathings; p. 16 © www.iStockphoto.com/Alexander Podshivalov; p. 18 © www.iStockphoto.com/Paulina Lenting-Smulders; p. 20 Mark S. Wexler/Getty Images.

Library of Congress Cataloging-in-Publication Data

Metz, Lorijo.
  Goats : nannies, billies, and kids / Lorijo Metz. — 1st ed.
    p. cm. — (On the farm)
  Includes index.
  ISBN 978-1-4488-0689-8 (library binding) — ISBN 978-1-4488-1339-1 (pbk.) — ISBN 978-1-4488-1340-7 (6-pack)
  1. Goats—Juvenile literature. I. Title. II. Series: Metz, Lorijo. On the farm.
  SF383.35.M48 2011
  636.3'9—dc22
                                          2010003470

Manufactured in the United States of America

CPSIA Compliance Information: Batch #WS10PK: For Further Information contact Rosen Publishing, New York, New York at 1-800-237-9932

Contents

Goats in Our World

If you ask for a glass of milk in the United States, you will likely get cow's milk. You might be surprised to learn that more people worldwide drink goat's milk than milk from a cow.

People have been keeping goats for over 9,000 years. Along with sheep, goats were one of the first kinds of animals to be **domesticated**. Today, some farmers raise

This goat is a billy goat, or male goat. Adult male goats sometimes have a strong smell.

Goats can live on many types of land, such as fields, deserts, and mountains. This makes it possible to raise them on farms in many places.

goats for meat or leather. Other farmers raise goats for dairy **products** such as milk and cheese. People also raise goats for wool. Some of the softest, most expensive clothing in the world is made from the wool of cashmere goats.

Farm Facts

People call male goats bucks or billy goats. Female goats are known as does or nanny goats. Baby goats are called kids!

5

What Do Goats Look Like?

Goats come in many sizes, from 20-pound (9 kg) Nigerian dwarf goats to 300-pound (136 kg) Boer goats. Some goats have long, curly hair. Others have short, straight hair.

As you can see from this photo, different goats can look very different from each other.

All goats have strong, two-toed hooves. These hooves help them cross rocky ground and even climb trees.

Almost all goats have **beards**. Farmers often trim the beards of nanny goats, though. Most, but not all, goats are born with horns. Goat horns are hollow. They curl back from a goat's head. While

The inside of a goat's horns is made of living bone. On the outside, goat horns have matter like that found in hair and fingernails!

goat horns are beautiful, they are also sharp. They can harm other goats. Goat horns can also get caught in fences. Many farmers choose to **disbud** baby goats shortly after they are born.

Those Clever, Curious Creatures

Goats are very curious, or interested in the world around them. They always want to know what is going on.

Goats are clever creatures. They are quick to learn good habits and just as quick to pick up bad ones. Once a goat has learned how to open a gate, there is no keeping it inside!

Goats are also good climbers. They can walk on top of fences or crawl under them. Goats can also jump over 5 feet (1.5 m) up!

Farm Facts

Many people believe goats eat tin cans. However, they are more likely to chew the paper off them.

This goat is high up in a tree! Many goats are skilled tree climbers. They are sure-footed and have an excellent sense of balance.

Curious goats will climb up trees and over mountains to find new **sources** of food. Some people say goats will eat anything. However, that is not true. They refuse to eat things that taste bad to them.

Breeds of Goats

Most modern goats are **descended** from the wild bezoar goat. Early people raised bezoar goats for food and clothing. They also used their bones and skin for building.

Today, there are many goat **breeds**. Some goats were bred for a certain use.

There are several kinds of wild goats. This wild goat is an Alpine ibex. Alpine ibexs live in a group of mountains in Europe, called the Alps.

For example, some breeds give lots of milk. The long, wide-eared Nubian goat and the small-eared LaMancha goat are two common breeds of dairy goats. Goats raised

10

Angora goats, such as the one here, are known for their long, soft, wavy wool. Angora goats originally came from Turkey.

for meat include the Spanish goat and the Boer goat. The Spanish goat is a strong, small breed. The Boer goat is larger and comes from South Africa. Other breeds, such as Angora goats, are raised for their wool.

These young goats are Nubian goats. Unlike most other goats, Nubian goats have big, floppy ears.

The Social Goat

Goats are social animals. This means that they prefer to live in groups with other goats. To **communicate**, goats bleat. Goats bleat if they are hungry or need attention. Nanny goats bleat to call their kids.

Goats pay a lot of attention to the world around them. They have good eyesight.

Though they are social animals, goats do not always get along. Goats sometimes fight by ramming into each other.

12

Along with their other sharp senses, goats have an excellent sense of smell. In fact, their sense of smell makes it very hard to sneak up on a goat!

They also have excellent hearing. They can hear a wide range of sounds, from the high-pitched cry of a kid to the low growl of a predator. A goat needs only to turn its ears to learn where the sound is coming from.

Farm Facts

A group of goats may be called a herd, a tribe, a flock, or a trip of goats.

This group of goats is spending a sunny day resting and eating in a meadow. Goats spend a lot of their time eating.

Goat Kids

Nanny goats are generally good mothers. When their kids get scared, mother goats nestle up to them to make them feel safer.

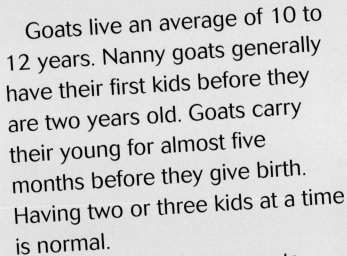

Goats live an average of 10 to 12 years. Nanny goats generally have their first kids before they are two years old. Goats carry their young for almost five months before they give birth. Having two or three kids at a time is normal.

The first thing nanny goats do after their kids are born is to lick them clean. This also helps

Farm Facts

The milk a newborn kid drinks during the first few hours of life is important. This milk, called colostrum, helps the newborn stay healthy as it grows.

This boy is feeding milk to a Nubian goat kid. If a goat kid's mother cannot care for it, the kid can be fed milk from a bottle.

the newborns breathe. Within half an hour, most kids are standing and drinking their mothers' milk. By the time they are 12 weeks old, most kids are ready to be **weaned**.

What Do Goats Eat?

Many people believe goats will eat anything, but they will not. Goats are herbivores. Herbivores eat only plants. Wild goats often lived in places where there were few plants. In order to find enough food, they learned to

As all animals do, goats need to drink clean water. This goat is drinking from a stream.

eat many different kinds of plants. Given the choice, goats prefer to eat leaves, bark, and flowers. They also eat fresh, green grass. Goats have a good sense of smell and will not eat anything that smells too old.

Like cows, goats are ruminants. Ruminants are hoofed animals that have special stomachs with four parts. This allows them to eat plants that need extra chewing to **digest**.

Goats often have to climb to reach their favorite foods, such as leaves and bark. Happily, they are very good at climbing!

If they are in a field, goats will eat small bushes and other plants before they eat grass.

Meat Goats and Dairy Goats

Many people who cannot drink cow's milk drink goat's milk instead. Unlike cow's milk, goat's milk does not need to be **homogenized**. Many of the cheeses made with goat's milk are called chèvre.

This kid is a Saanen goat. Saanen goats are most often raised for their milk. The first Saanen goats came from the Saanen Valley, in Switzerland.

Chèvres are often soft and easy to spread. The Italian cheese *caprino* is made with goat's milk, too. People also make goat's milk yogurt and even goat's milk ice cream.

There are many kinds of cheese made from goat's milk. This goat's milk cheese is called *sirene*. It is often eaten in Bulgaria.

As is the case with goat's milk, more people worldwide eat goat meat than cow meat. Goat meat is also called chevon. It is common in Mexican, Indian, and Greek cooking. Chevon is low in fat and high in **protein**.

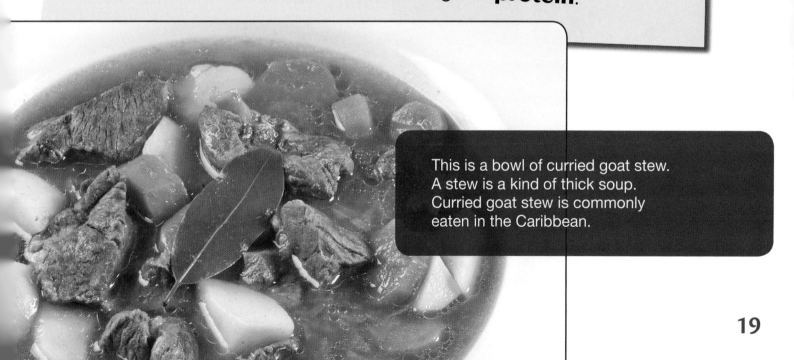
This is a bowl of curried goat stew. A stew is a kind of thick soup. Curried goat stew is commonly eaten in the Caribbean.

19

Angora and Cashmere Goats

Though Angora goats arrived in the United States only in 1849, the country is now one of the world's largest angora producers. Angora goats produce a **fiber** called mohair. Mohair has many uses. Blankets, rugs, and children's toys can all be made from mohair. It is also used to make clothing for both warm and cold weather.

This Angora goat has just been shorn, or had its wool cut off. You can see the pile of mohair from it next to the goat.

Cashmere is a soft, warm fiber. It has been called the Fiber of Kings. Most of the world's cashmere comes from China. Unlike Angora goats, cashmere goats are a type, not a breed. Dairy goats, such as the Saanen goat, and meat goats, such as the Spanish meat goat, both have the fine **undercoat** used for cashmere.

These cashmere goats are in Kashmir. Kashmir is an area that includes parts of India, Pakistan, and China. Though the words are spelled differently, cashmere gets its name from Kashmir.

Goats Are Here to Stay!

People have found many uses for goats. Goat hides make beautiful rugs and fine leather. Other parts of the goat are made into such things as soap and pet food.

In places like the Himalayas, people have used goats as pack

This girl is visiting a goat at a petting zoo. Goats can often be found in petting zoos.

animals for thousands of years. Not only are goats strong, they are also excellent climbers. Goats are easy to raise since they can live on brush and weeds. For so many reasons, the clever, curious goat is here to stay!

Glossary

beards (BIRDZ) Hair that grows on the face and chin.

breeds (BREEDZ) Groups of animals that look alike and have the same relatives.

communicate (kuh-MYOO-nih-kayt) To share facts or feelings.

descended (dih-SEN-did) Born of a certain family or group.

digest (dy-JEST) To break down food so that the body can use it.

disbud (dis-BUD) To remove the horns from.

domesticated (duh-MES-tih-kayt-id) Raised to live with people.

fiber (FY-ber) Something that can be spun into yarn.

homogenized (hoh-MAH-jeh-nyzd) Treated to be the same throughout.

products (PRAH-dukts) Things that are produced.

protein (PROH-teen) An important element inside the cells of plants and animals.

sources (SORS-ez) Places from which things come.

undercoat (UN-der-koht) A soft coat of wool that is under a longer coat.

weaned (WEEND) Changed a baby's food from a mother's milk to solid food.

Index

B
beards, 7

C
cheese, 5, 18
chevon, 19
chèvre, 18
clothing, 5, 10, 20

E
ears, 13

F
farmers, 4–5, 7
fiber, 20–21

food, 9–10, 16, 22

H
hair, 6
herbivores, 16
hooves, 6
horns, 7

L
leather, 5, 22

M
milk, 4–5, 10, 15,
    18–19
mohair, 20

P
protein, 19

R
ruminants, 17

S
sources, 9

U
undercoat, 21

W
weeds, 22
wool, 5, 11

Web Sites

Due to the changing nature of Internet links, PowerKids Press has developed an online list of Web sites related to the subject of this book. This site is updated regularly. Please use this link to access the list:
www.powerkidslinks.com/otf/goats/